52 WEEKS

OF FAMILY

FRENCH

Eileen Mc Aree

DEDICATION

This book is dedicated to Sheila.

You are the best sister and friend in the world.

CONTENTS

Introduction

Learning a foreign language is a wonderful goal, and it can also be a fun and rewarding experience. What stops many people from attempting to learn a foreign language is their own fear of speaking, of looking foolish in front of another person. They may be comfortable studying vocabulary lists or grammar rules, but without actually speaking a language, no one can really progress. *52 Weeks of Family French* is designed to get you speaking French from the very first day!

Not only will you build on your own success as you learn to communicate in French, you will take your children along on this exciting journey. Children are naturally curious and full of enthusiasm. They haven't yet faced a conjugated verb or a double negative. They have no idea that learning to speak a foreign language is supposed to be difficult. What better study partners could you ask for? For most of us, our inhibitions about pronouncing foreign words disappear when we practice with our children. Using the simple lessons provided in this book, you and your children will be speaking to each other (and hopefully other people) in French quickly and easily.

52 Weeks of Family French is designed to be a relaxed, self-teaching guide. Each week you focus on a simple conversational concept that you and your children can practice together. The conversations were chosen based on their relevance to real, everyday family life. The lessons are short and simple and will get you and your family practicing French in the many of the moments modern families share together: mealtimes, morning "rush hour", carpools, bedtime. This is an oral introduction to the French language, so there are no spelling rules to memorize or flashcards to flip. Grammar is touched on throughout the curriculum but the main goal is to get you and your family speaking this beautiful language.

Features of the Book

Before you begin, take a look through the book. There are several features that will make the learning process easier for both you and your children.

- ## Words and Phrases to Get You Started
  This is a small compilation of some words and phrases you should know from the beginning to encourage and instruct your children.

- ## 52 Week Curriculum

  This is the heart of it all, and when you see how simple each week's lesson is, you may be surprised. Certain weeks focus on only one phrase! The fact is that fifty-two small, achievable lessons add up to quite a store of conversational skills, and conversation is the ultimate goal of this book. It was written to provide a family with a respectable oral vocabulary in about a year. Exactly how fast your family progresses is entirely up to you. If you and your kids are in a groove and you want to move ahead, by all means follow the momentum. On the other hand, if you are dealing with an ear infection, an impending dance recital and a huge deadline at work, stretch one week's lesson into three weeks. The pace is yours to decide. You and your family will be successful if you simply *keep talking.*

- Suggested Activities

As every busy parent knows, it is not always easy to find time to go to the supermarket, let alone learn *and teach* a brand new language. This section is full of realistic, fun and engaging ways to practice your French skills in the context of your everyday life.

- Resources

Listed here are many wonderful materials available to make learning a foreign language fun and engaging. The internet makes it possible to access many educational games for free. For those with "smart" phones, there are apps that can reinforce language learning while you wait outside school, in a fast food pick up line, or entertain a younger sibling at baseball practice. Also listed here are some books and CD's that can further pique your child's interest in the French language.

How to Use This Book

1. **52 Weeks of Family French** follows an auditory and oral learning model. Listening to the sounds of a new language and communicating successfully in that language opens the mind to a new structure of thinking. Vocabulary drills and grammar rules shut down the learning process at this early stage. This is not to imply vocabulary and grammar are not crucial to the mastery of any language. It is simply that to get the process started, *the natural way is to start talking.*

2. **Talk, Talk, Talk!** Use your new vocabulary every day, even it is only for a one minute conversation. You will be surprised and pleased to see how a minimal time commitment, *every day*, leads to the attainment of a great deal of vocabulary.

3. **Watch your pronunciation.** Try to correct any major pronunciation errors as soon as they occur. The pronunciation guides should help you with this. The faster you correct yourself, the faster you will learn.

4. **Touch on each week's** *cultural note.* Every week's lesson includes a fact about a country or culture where French is spoken. Introducing children to different French cultures increases their curiosity about the

language. It makes the process more interesting and fun for you as well!

5. **Take time to review**. Review weeks are built into the curriculum. Take your time! If you feel you and your family haven't mastered one week's concept, continue your review till you are ready to move on.

6. **Remember, it's a journey, not a race**. Many language courses advertise mastery of a language in record time. Babies don't learn to talk overnight, and people don't speak new languages overnight either. Your French speaking skills will continue to improve as long as you keep speaking and learning. Enjoy!

Suggested Activities

1. **Short and sweet conversations**. Each week's lesson is bite size French concept that you can review during a five minute conversation. Resist the impulse to drill, if your child forgot a word, just provide it for them. The repetition of language will help their vocabulary grow. Great places for bite-sized conversations are:

    - In the car...all parents spend plenty of time in the car! Use this time to squeeze in some language learning.

    - At mealtimes...many of the lessons in this book are perfect to review before breakfast, lunch or dinner...or snack at the pool...or a snack in the mall.....

    - Bedtimes...start with "Je t'aime"" and move on from there!

    - "Downtime"...Waiting in the pediatrician's examination room, waiting for your food to be delivered at Chili's, anytime or place you need to kill five minutes, use it to review French!

2. **Put on the radio.** By putting on French language CD or podcast in the car or kitchen while you make dinner, you acclimate your ear, and your children's if they are listening, to the rhythm and cadence of French speech. You are

hearing native or fluent speakers provide an accent model as well.

3. **Find a French language children's TV show.** Children's television shows are not terribly complicated in terms of character and plot, and you can derive meaning just by watching. Many local cable companies offer a French channel for an additional (modest) charge.

4. **Read a bilingual storybook.** In the Resources section of this book, I list websites that can help you locate children's picture books in both English and French. The plots are simple so you can get a lot of meaning from the picture clues. Also, reading aloud to your children helps you work on your accent.

5. **Say hello!** One of the hardest parts of learning a new language is overcoming our own embarrassment and communicating with native speakers. If you can get over this hurdle you will have conquered a challenge that turns many people away from learning a second language. In certain areas of the world, it may be easy to meet French speaking people. In others, it is difficult to find anyone who speaks French at all. Utilize the internet to locate groups of fellow Francophiles.

6. **Make friends.** One of the benefits of being learning about a new culture and language is meeting new friends. Whether you meet a local mother who hails from Paris or you need to utilize the internet to find language partners, you will surely enrich your life with the new and interesting people you will meet.

7. **Start a playgroup.** If you are a take charge kind of person, start your own playgroup! No matter where in the world you live, you can guarantee there are other parents

interested in teaching their children French. Internet sites like Meetup.com are great tools for creating playgroups.

8. **Play.** Have fun with French. The Resources section lists lots of fun games, books and CD's to support your learning. In addition, try playing the following vocabulary review games with your kids:

- *Où est-ce?* Ask your children where different items in the room are. They recognize the vocabulary word and point to the item.

- *Chaud ou froid?* This is your basic game of hot or cold except instead of hiding an object in the room, you *think* of an item in the room. You then direct your children toward it with cues of *chaud ou froid.* The child who figures out which item you were thinking of (lamp, television, etc.) must call out the name of the item in French.

- *Maman (Papa) dit, "Touche ton/ta/tes.."* Here is a version of Simon says. Mommy (or Daddy) says to touch different body parts, items in the room, items of clothing etc. Children must understand the vocabulary they are hearing in order to act accordingly. They are out if they touch something and Mama didn't say!

- *Vingt questions.* Children are given the opportunity to ask twenty questions to figure out the item you are thinking of. They can ask questions about it in English (or French as their knowledge increases) but they have to guess what it is in French.

- *Je vois quelque chose…* Play this game the same way you would play *I Spy.* As your vocabulary increases you can use more and more French describing words to help your children puzzle out what you see.

- ***Puppets.*** Puppets are an invaluable tool for teaching language. Buy or make a hand puppet, name your puppet (Try French names to go with your theme!), and make the puppet your French teacher's helper. Anytime you want to review dialog, take out your puppet and talk away. Older children can help put on the puppet show for younger children.

- ***Beanbag Toss***. This is simply another way to review vocabulary. Get a beanbag (or soft, small ball, or stuffed animal, anything that won't go through a window or cause a concussion). The first person says a word or phrase in French and tosses the beanbag to the next person who then has to give the translation. If they don't get the correct answer, they are out. If they do get the correct answer, they come up with another French phrase and toss the beanbag to the next person. You can reverse this activity and say the words or phrases in English and have the children provide the French translation. That is always a little harder!

Words and Phrases to Get You Started

As an individual, you are embarking on a journey to learn French. As a parent, you are additionally taking on the role of teacher. With this knowledge in mind, prepare yourself from day one with some basic vocabulary that will guide and encourage your children. It also adds to the language they will pick up through exposure!

Très bien!:   Very good!

Fantastique!:   Fantastic!

Merveilleux!:   Wonderful!

Dis- le moi encore une fois: Tell me again.

Répète, s'il te plaît: Repeat, please.

Essaie encore: Try again.

Sois attentif!:   Pay attention!

Calme-toi: Calm down.

Attends: Wait.

Viens ici: Come here.

Beau travail!:   Good job!

Écoute-moi: Listen to me.

Dans une seconde…:   In a second….

And don't forget……*Je t'aime:*   I love you!

52 Week Curriculum

Here is an overview of how the weeks of your year of learning French are divided. Topics were chosen for ease of learning and application to real life. Suggested reviews are included in each week's lesson. Don't feel compelled to go in order! If you want to learn how to say, "I'm hungry!" in French, by all means skip straight to Unit 5. Remember, go in an order that is interesting to you and at a speed you and your family are comfortable with. This book was written to make French learning easy and fun!

Unit 1: Weeks 1-8
Theme: Making Friends
Cultural Spotlight: Introducing France

Unit 2: Weeks 9-16
Theme: All About Me
Cultural Spotlight: A Child's Life in France

Unit 3: Weeks 17-24
Theme: Welcome to My Home
Cultural Spotlight: French Art and Music

Unit 4: Weeks 25-32
Theme: Useful Information
Cultural Spotlight: French Food

Unit 5: Weeks 33-40
Theme: Mealtimes
Cultural Spotlight: Famous French People

Unit 6: 41-48
Theme: Getting Ready
Cultural Spotlight: French Culture Around the World

Unit 7: Weeks 49-52
Theme: A Few Odds and Ends
Cultural Spotlight: Fun French Facts!

Unit 1: Making Friends

Week 1: Manners

Vocabulary:

oui/non *wee/noh*	(yes/no)
s'il-vous plait *sil voo play*	(please)
merci *mair-see*	(thanks)
merci beaucoup *mair-see boh-ku*	(thank you very much)
de rien *duh- ree -ehn*	(you're welcome)

Pronunciation note: The vowel sounds in French differ widely from the vowel sounds in English. Try to listen to spoken French to hear the differences.

Cultural Note: France is one of the largest countries in Europe. It has many beautiful areas: majestic mountain ranges, lovely countryside and beaches that are visited by tourists from around the world. Don't forget..France also contains historic cities that are world centers of culture and business like Paris, Lyon and Marseille.

Idea! Use your new manners words at mealtimes. Pair the English word of whatever you want with the French manners word. Encourage your children to do the same. Don't worry about mixing up the languages, that's how communication is born.

Week 2: Greetings

Review: Week 1: Manners

Vocabulary:

salut *sah-lew*	(hello)
au revoir *oh-rhe-vwahr*	(goodbye)
bonjour *bohn-jhoor*	(Good morning)
bonsoir *bohn-swahr*	(Good evening)

Pronunciation note:. Sometimes in French, the letters are written but remain silent. Remember to drop the final consonant in *salut*.

Cultural Note: The capital of France is Paris, but there are 22 regions within the country. To travel within the country, people can take high speed trains called TGV's, *trains à grande vitesse.*

Idea! In France, it is very important for children to learn to greet others with "*bonjour*" and tell them "*au revoir*" as they leave. Adopt this French nicety by teaching your kids to not only say "please" and "thank you", but "hello" and "goodbye" to adults they encounter. Saying it in French is bonus!

Week 3: Introductions

Review: Week 2: Greetings

Vocabulary:

Comment allez-vous? *koh-mahn-tah-lay-voo*	(How are you)
Je vais bien. *jhuh-vay-byahn*	(good)
Et vous? *ay-voo*	(and you?)

Grammar note:. Often in spoken French, the words flow into each other. In French this is known as *enchainement*. Do your best to follow the pronunciation guide when learning new phrases and don't "chop" the sounds up word by word.

Cultural Note: Paris is one of the most famous and popular cities in the world. Some Parisian landmarks that you may have heard of are: the Eiffel Tower, The Arc de Triomphe, the Sorbonne, the Notre Dame de Paris, and the Louvre. There are many cultural and historic attractions in Paris, a city also known as "the City of Light".

Idea! Have fun role playing out a simple conversation with your children.

Bonjour. Comment allez-vous?

Je vais bien, merci. Et vous?

Bien, merci.

Week 4: What's Your Name?

Review: Week 2: Greetings

Vocabulary:

Comment vous appelez vous? (What is your name ?)
koh-mahn-voo-ah-pehl-lay-voo

Je m'appelle_____. (My name is_____.)
jhuh-mah-pehl_____.

Pronunciation note: There is a formal you, *vous,* and an informal you, *tu,* in French. Since you don't know a stranger, here we are using the formal you, *vous.*

Cultural note: Another famous area of France is Provence. In Provence you can find fields of lavender, as far as the eye can see. Many of these purple flowers used for perfumes.

Idea! Velvet rope your kitchen! Before dinner or other mealtime where you are not too rushed, hang a streamer across the kitchen door and before children can enter they must answer the question, *"Comment vous appelez vous?".*

Week 5: How Old Are You?

Review: Week 4: What is Your Name?

Vocabulary:

Quel âge as-tu?   (How old are you?)
kehl-hajh-ah-too

J'ai_____ans.   (I am _____ years old.)
jhay_____ahn

Pronunciation note: The letter "j" in French produces a sound somewhere between an English *j*, a *z* and *sh*. Throughout this book, it is referred to as *jh* within the pronunciation guide. The best thing you can do is listen to spoken French the proper sound.

Cultural Note: Have you ever heard of Champagne? Well it is not just a drink, it is the name of the region in which it is made! Other popular wine growing regions are Burgundy and Bordeaux

Idea! Teach your child the French number for their age. Then interview each other as if you just met using the vocabulary from the previous lessons. Siblings can interview each other!

Week 6: More Greetings

Review: Week 3, Introductions

Vocabulary:

Comment ça va?   (How's it going?)
koh-mahn-sah-vah

Et toi?   (and you?)
ay-twah

A bientôt!   (See you soon!)
ah-byehn-toh

Grammar note: In French, there is a formal and informal way to address others. In Week 2, you learned the formal way to greet neighbors, coworkers or the way children would address adults. *"Comment ça va?"* is the more relaxed way of greeting one another. You could say this to friends or people you feel comfortable with. *Tu* is the informal way of saying you.

Cultural note: France's lengthy borders touch many other European countries: Belgium and Germany in the north, Spain in the South, Switzerland and Italy in the east. No wonder France is often referred to as the center of Europe!

Idea! Incorporate these new phrases into your everyday life. *"Comment ça va?"* can be used every day while checking to see how the kid's homework is coming along. *"A bientôt!"* is a great way to say goodbye before leaving for work in the morning.

Week 7: Nice to Meet You!

Review: Week 4: What's Your Name?

Vocabulary:

> Enchantée   (It's nice to meet you!)
> *ahn-shahn-tay*

Grammar note: There is a spelling difference when this phrase is used for a male or a female speaker. The pronunciation remains the same for both.

Cultural note: With its natural attractions, beautiful cities and historic and cultural landmarks, France wins the spot of most popular vacation spot in the world! More than 75 million people visit France every year.

Idea! Let your family pretend they have never met. They can make up new names and ages. Let them experiment with the conversational phrases they learned in the last few weeks. Make sure they end their role play conversations with, *"Enchantée!"*.

Week 8: Review

- **Review:** all basic conversational vocabulary.

    o Use dolls or puppets to role play introductions.

- It can be challenging in some parts of the world to find people with whom to speak French. Try posting a notice at your local library for French study buddies (children or adults!). You will see that there are Francophiles located in every corner of the globe!

- Learn more about France!

    o Go to a French restaurant.
    o Read about the Concorde – the fastest commercial plane in the world.
    o Go to a department store and smell some French perfume.
    o Utilize the internet to "tour" some of the famous sights of Paris.
    o Color in a French flag.
    o The French are avid sports fans. Research what French sports are current. Watch a French soccer game online, view the Tour de France or see a tennis match. Look on the Internet and watch *boules*. Or if you are feeling active, get out and play some handball – the French are handball champs!

Unit 2: All About Me

Week 9: Who Am I?

Review: Basic conversation from Week 1-8.
Vocabulary:

> Qui êtes-vous?   (Who are you?)
> *Keet voo*
>
> Je suis une fille.   (I am a girl.)
> *jhuh-swee-ewn-fee-yuh*
>
> Je suis un garçon.(I am a boy.)
> *jhuh-swee-uhn-gar-sohn*
>
> Je suis _____.   (I am *insert child's name.*)
> *jhuh-swee_____.*

Grammar note: When speaking French, words change depending on gender. Here we use the article *une* when we are talking about a girl. We use the article *un* when we are talking about a boy.

Cultural note: Students in France have a long school day- typically 8:30-4:00! There may also be classes Saturday mornings, but students usually have off on Wednesdays.

Idea! Take turns answering the question, *"Qui êtes-vous?"*. Encourage your children to also use previously learned vocabulary (ex: it would also be appropriate to respond, Je

22

m'appelle_____). If your children would like to expand on the lesson, look up the translation of something he or she loves to do.

Examples: *Je suis danseuse :* I am a dancer.
                  Je suis artiste: I am an artist.

Remember to watch your use of gender!

Week 10: Feelings

Review: Week 3: Introductions
Vocabulary:

> Je suis content(e).   (I am happy.)
> *jhuh-swee-kohn-tah*

> Je me sens triste.   (I am sad.)
> *jhuh-meh-sahns-treest*

The female ending is in parentheses.

Grammar note: The French *r* is completely different from the English *r*. The French *r* sound comes from the back of the throat, where we make the sound *k*. Try it, you may sound at first like you are saying *gr*. Practice the French *r* sound with your children every day. You will improve and you will all have a laugh while you are at it!

Cultural note: Many schools in France have what is known as *classe de neige* (class in the snow) or *classe de mer* (class by the sea). The whole class goes together on a vacation to either a winter resort or the beach. Don't think it's all fun and no work though, classes go on as usual, with lots of extra fun activities mixed in.

Idea! Have your children make exaggerated faces while they say in French whether they are happy or sad

Week 11: What Do I Look Like?

Review: Week 9: Who Am I?

Vocabulary:

Je suis *jhuh-swee*	(I am)
grand(e) *grahn*	(tall)
petit(e) *puh-tee*	(short)
jolie *jhoh-lee*	(pretty)
beau *boo*	(handsome)

Grammar note: Adjectives are typically presented with both the male and female endings. You decide which ending to use based on who or what you are describing.

Example: *Le garçon est grand.* (The boy is tall.)

La fille est grande. (The girl is tall.)

Cultural note: The French are animal lovers! Many children in France have a family pet. France has the highest number of pet owners in Europe. In Paris, there are more dogs than children!

Idea! Use your cell phone to call your house phone. Let your kids chat to one another, greeting each other and describing themselves in French.

Week 12: What Do I Look Like?

Review: Week 11: What Do I Look Like?

Vocabulary:

> J'ai les cheveux blonds.   (I have blond hair.)
> *jhay-lay-shoo-voo-bluhn*

> J'ai les cheveux bruns.   (I have brown hair)
> *jhay-lay-shoo-voo-brah*

> J'ai les cheveux roux.   (I have red hair.)
> *jhay-lay-shoo-voo-roojh*

> J'ai les cheveux noirs.   (I have black hair.)
> *jhay-lay-shoo-voo-nwah*

Grammar note: French words have to match in gender and also in number. If you are talking about more than one noun, all the describing words attached to it must also show that it is more than one.

Cultural note: Mealtimes are important in France, and the whole family typically eats together, and eats the same food! There are no "kids foods" in France. Children eat the same delicious, healthy food as adults.

Idea! Have your children draw a self portrait. They can then use their new vocabulary to describe what they have drawn.

Week 13: What I Like to Do

Review: Weeks 11-12: What Do I Look Like?

Vocabulary:

Qu' est-ce que tu aimes faire?   (What do you like to do ?)
kays-kuh-too-ehm-fayr

J'aime lire   (I like to read.)
jhehm leer

J'aime nager   (I like to swim.)
jhehm –neh-jhay

Grammar note: Verbs are words that tell about things we can do. We add a verb to the phrase *J'aime* to tell what we like to do.

Cultural note: All children in France play sports. French schools are very concerned with physical fitness, *la forme.*

Idea! Have each child pick their own activity they like to do (not listed above). Help them look up the French verb online or in a French dictionary and make their own sentence. Suggestions: *danser (to dance), chanter (to sing), jouer au football (to play soccer), jouer sur l'ordinateur (to play on the computer).*

Week 14: My Face

Review: Weeks 11 and 12: What Do I Look Like?:

Vocabulary:

Touchez ton/ta/tes….	(Touch your…)
(le) nez *luh nay*	(nose)
(le) visage *luh vee-sahj*	(face)
(la) bouche *lah boosh*	(mouth)
(les) yeux *lay yuh*	(eyes)
(les) oreilles *lay ohr-ay*	(ears)

Pronunciation note: In French, when we use the word "your", we have to decide whether to be familiar or formal. Here we are using the familiar "your". However, you still have to match your pronoun "your" to the object's gender and number. For this reason, You would say, *Touchez ton nez* (male, singular). *Touchez ta bouche* (female, singular), and *Touchez tes yeux* (plural). Don't worry if you mix up your pronouns at this early stage of learning, but try and practice "matching" the right form of "your" with different parts of the face.

Cultural note: French children like to watch TV just like American children. In France, cartoons are called, *les dessins animés.*

Idea! Play a version of "Simon Says" called "Maman Dit". This is a game you can play anywhere to review vocabulary. "Maman dit: touchez ton nez!" Remember, if Maman didn't say…you are out!

Week 15: My Body

Review: Week 14: My Face

Vocabulary:

(la) tête   (head)
lah teht

(le) bras   (arm)
luh brah

(le) pied   (foot)
luh pee-eh

(la) jambe   (leg)
lah-jzahm

(la) main   (hand)
lah mehn

Pronunciation note: Remember, ê is pronounced like *eh*.

Cultural note: Children in France are expected to be well mannered at a very young age. Parents monitor their children closely to make sure they know how to behave at mealtimes, in public and with adults.

Idea! Expand on your "Maman Dit" game to include parts of the body.

Week 16: Review

- Review all vocabulary from the past eight weeks.

  o Role play conversations
  o Draw self portraits and describe
  o Point out other people and pretend to be them. How would they describe themselves?

- Learn more about French family life.

  o Make a *coq au vin* for dinner. It sounds fancy, but it is actually a French chicken stew. This famous dish originated as peasant food and has lasted throughout the years because of its delicious, hearty flavors. Healthy and delicious!
  o Go to the supermarket to find French cheeses and make a sampler platter for an afterschool snack.
  o Introduce your children to the world of Tintin by Hergé. These famous French cartoon books will awaken the adventurer in child!
  o Get out the chalk and play "Escargot", a traditional French children's game. Draw a shape like a giant snail and fill with 15 to 20 numbered squares, leading toward the center. Children must hop to the center square without landing on any lines or claimed squares. If they make it, they get to choose their own square to initial. Whoever claims the most squares wins the game.

Unit 3: Welcome to My Home

Week 17: Welcome to My Home

Review: Weeks 9-16

Vocabulary:

> Bienvenu(es) chez moi! (Welcome to my home!)
> *byah-veh-noo-shay-mwah*

Pronunciation note: Many vowel sounds in French are *nasal*, which means you push air out of your mouth and nose without the use of your lips, tongue or throat. Try this sound with *moi*.

Cultural note: France has been a traditional center for the creation of art and music. Many of the great art movements have originated in France, like Romanticism, Impressionism and Fauvism.

Idea! Take the plunge! Invite someone over, drum up your courage and welcome them in French. If you feel corny, don't worry. The more you use your French, the more natural it feels.

Week 18: Where Is It?

Review: Week 17: Welcome to my home!

Vocabulary:

Où est….. ?   (Where is……?)
oo-ay

la salle de bain   (bathroom)
lah sahl duh bahn

la cuisine   (kitchen)
lah kwee-zeen

Grammar note: Remember, all French nouns are masculine or feminine. Is *la salle* masculine or feminine? How about *la cuisine*?

Cultural note: Paul Cézanne is one of the most famous painters from France. His work influenced many artists in later years. Utilize Google Images to see some of his famous works like, *The Black Marble Clock.*

Idea! Practice using *"Où est…?"* with words you already know. This is a quick and easy way to practice.

"Où est (insert your child's name)?"

"Où est ton nez?"

Week 19: Where Is _____?

Review: Week 18: Where Is... ?

Vocabulary:

la table	(table)
lah tahb	
la chaise	(chair)
lah shehz	
la porte	(door)
lah pohrt	
la fenêtre	(window)
lah fuh-neht-ruh	

Pronunciation note: Remember the *e* at the end of a French word is mute, or not pronounced.

Cultural note: The Louvre is one of the most famous art museums in the world. People come from every country on Earth to see the artistic masterpieces it contains. Some paintings you may have heard of at the Louvre are the *Mona Lisa* by Leonardo da Vinci and *The Lacemaker* by Johannes Vermeer. There are also world class exhibitions of antiquities, decorative arts and sculptures.

Idea! Have a treasure hunt! Hide some prizes (something small, an m&m, or sticker) in spots around your house. Say; *"Où est la table?"* for example, and let your child claim the prize when they find the right object.

Week 20: Meet My Family (A)

Review: Week 19: Where is it?

Vocabulary:

C'est mon père. (This is my father.)
say-mohn-payr

C'est ma mère. (This is my mother.)
say-mah-mayr

Grammar note:. *C'est* is a very important phrase as it can mean, "it is", "this is", or "that is" depending on the context of the sentence.

Cultural note: Claude Monet is one of the most famous painters in the world. He lived during the nineteenth century and was one of the leaders of the Impressionist movement. His beautiful colors and light filled paintings remain popular to this day.

Idea! At dinner let your kids have fun presenting their mom or dad.

Week 21: Meet My Family (B)

Review: Week 20: Meet My Family (A)

Vocabulary:

> Qui est-ce? (Who is this?)
> *kee-ehs*

> C'est mon frère. (This is my brother.)
> *say-mohn-frayr*

> C'est ma sœur. (This is my sister.)
> *say-mah-suhr*

Pronunciation note: There are vowel combinations in French that simply do not exist in English. The symbol *œ* represents a joined vowel sound, similar to an English *ooh*.

Cultural note: Although ballet originated in Italy, classical ballet as we know it today was developed in France. This is the reason so many ballet terms are in French: *ballet, arabesque, coupé, jeté and plié* to name a few.,

Idea! Car practice: Have your children take turns "introducing" everyone in the car .

Week 22: Meet My Family (C)

Review: Weeks 20 and 21:Meet My Family (A and B)

Vocabulary:

        la grand-mère   (grandmother)
        lah grahn-mehr

        le grand-père   (grandfather)
        luh grahn-pehr

        la tante   (aunt)
        lah tahnt

        l'oncle   (uncle)
        luh-nonk

        le/la cousin(e)   (cousin)
        luh koo-zehn/lah koo-zeen

Pronunciation note: The *e* is dropped from the word *le* to form the contraction *l'oncle*. In French this is done often and affects the pronunciation of the two words.

Cultural note: Claude Debussy was a famous French composer who lived in the eighteenth century. He was a brilliant pianist but argued with a lot of people! Even so, his determination to follow his own way led to some of the most beautiful musical compositions of his time.

Idea! Go through your family album and identify members of your family in French.

Week 23: His Name Is_____.

Review: Weeks 20-22: Meet My Family (A,B,C)

Vocabulary:

>Je m'appelle...   (My name is...)
>*jhuh-mah-pehl*

>Il s'appelle...   (His name is...)
>*ills-ah-pehl*

>Elle s'appelle... (Her name is...)
>*ehls-ah-pehl*

Grammar note:. Sometimes the phrasing in another language is different than what we are used to in English. In French, we are literally saying, "He is called..." or "She is called..". However, when learning a new language, always translate for meaning. In English we would phrase this as, "His name is....".

Cultural note: France is also famous for its varied styles of architecture. One notable example is the Arc de Triomphe, a famous French landmark. France was the first country to have a university devoted to architecture, the Academy of Architecture. This academy was founded in 1671 and continues on to this day, as part of the modern French Institute.

Idea! Go around the dinner table and tell your own name and the name of the person on the right.

Week 24: Review

- Review vocabulary and concepts from weeks 17-23.

  - Now you have the phrases, " Touche ton/ta/tes...." and "Où est...?" under your belt. These are two of the quickest ways to do impromptu reviews anywhere! Use them whenever you think of them.
  - Throw an old magazine in your car. When you have some wait time at pick ups or drop offs, ask kids to point to la table, la porte, etc
  - Have a camera phone or digital camera? Let your kids scroll through the pictures as long as they are verbally labeling all the family members they see.

- Learn more about the arts in France!

  - Get a book on the Impressionists out from the library.
  - Look up images of the beautiful varied examples of French architecture.
  - Listen to a CD of Debussy or Ravel as you get ready for bed.
  - Watch a performance of George Balanchine's ballets on YouTube.
  - Read about the Palace of Versailles.
  - Have a budding ballerina in your family? Translate her positions from French to English.

Unit 4: Useful Information

Week 25: Days of the Week

Review: Review Weeks 17-24

Vocabulary:

lundi　　　(Monday)
loohn-dee

mardi　　　(Tuesday)
mahr-dee

mercredi　(Wednesday)
meh-kruh-dee

jeudi　　　(Thursday)
jhoo-dee

vendredi　(Friday)
vahnd-ruh-dee

samedi　　(Saturday)
sah-muh-dee

dimanche　(Sunday)
dee-mahnsh

Grammar note: The days of the week in French are not capitalized as they are in English.

Example: *Aujourd'hui c'est lundi.* (Today is Monday.)

Cultural note: **Idea!** Write the days of the week on index cards and put them all in an envelope. Let your children take turns taking out the correct day of the week and hanging it on the fridge with a magnet.

Week 26: What Day is Today?

Review: Week 25: Days of the Week

Vocabulary:

        Quel jour sommes-nous?   (What day is today?)
        kehl-jhoor-sohm-noo

Grammar note: This is another example of why we translate for meaning, not word for word. When you say, "What day is it?" in French, you are literally saying, " What day are we?". Different words, but the same meaning.

Cultural note: Do you enjoy an afterschool snack? In France, that is called the "*goûter*". It is the only snack of the day and is really a small meal to hold children over till their dinner, which is typically served late. French people take nutrition seriously and believe in only eating at mealtimes…no little snacks all day!

Idea! Ask your kids each morning before they start their day, *"Quel jour sommes-nous?"*

Week 27:Numbers 1-10

Review: Week 5: How Old Are You?

Vocabulary:

zéro   (zero)
zay-roh

un   (one)
uh

deux   (two)
duh

trois   (three)
twah

quatre   (four)
kaht-ruh

cinq   (five)
sahnk

six   (six)
sees

sept   (seven)
seht

huit   (eight)
wheet

neuf   (nine)
nuhf

dix   (ten)
dees

Pronunciation note: Remember that the *h* in *huit* is silent.

Cultural note: There are between 350 to 400 different types of cheeses produced in France! Popular ones you may have tried are camembert, munster or brie de meaux.

Idea! Use playing card to help kids memorize their numbers. Hold up a card and if the child says the correct number in French, they get to keep the card. Make the joker worth *zéro* and the jack, queen and king worth *dix*.

Week 28: How Many?

Review: Week 27: Numbers 0-10

Vocabulary:

> Combien?   (How many?)
> *kohm-byahn*

Grammar note: In order to be able to speak any language, you need to know key question words. Now you can add *combien* to your existing repertoire of *qui, qu'es-ce quet, où, quand, quel* and *comment.* You can get quite a lot of information with these simple words!

Cultural note: Children in France often have croissants or bread rolls with hot chocolate for breakfast. You can buy bread from the supermarket, but most French people prefer to buy their bread from the *boulangerie*, the local bakery.

Idea! Review previous vocabulary through counting. *Combien fenêtres? Combien garçons?*

Week 29: Months

Review: Week 25: Days of the Week

Vocabulary:

janvier (January)
jahn-vee-ay

février (February)
fay-vree-ay

mars (March)
mahr

avril (April)
ah-vreel

mai (May)
may

juin (June)
jwehn

juillet (July)
jwee-ay

août (August)
ah-oot

septembre (September)
sehp-tahm-bruh

octobre (October)
ohk-toh-bruh

novembre (November)
noh-vahm-bruh

décembre   (December)
day-sahm-bruh

Grammar note: As you have probably noted from previous lessons, many words are the same in both French and English, just with different pronunciation. Other words are extremely similar. As a matter of fact, a large percentage of the English language has French origins. So you already know more French than you think!

Cultural Note: Sharing and enjoying food is a huge part of French culture. A French dinner will often have several courses: *hors d'œuvre*, which is a served before you sit at the table, a starter like soup, the *entrée,* a *plat principal*, the main dish and cheese or fruit to finish off the meal.

Idea! Many French names for the months sound similar to their English counterparts. Use this similarity to help your kids memorize them. Give your children a clue and they have to guess the month you are talking about in English:

Clue: The flowers bloom in *mai.* Answer: May

Clue: We fly kites in *mars.* Answer: March

Week 30: I Know.....

Review: Weeks 25 & 29: Days and Months of the Year

Vocabulary:

Je connai...   (I know...)
jhuh-kohn-neh

les jours de la semaine!   (the days of the week!)
lay jhoor duh lah suh-mehn

les mois de l'année!   (the months of the year)
lay mwah duh lah-nay

Grammar note: You have probably already noted the large number of contractions in the French phrases you are learning. We have contractions in English as well, but in French they are part of the formal language rules. Since we are focusing on *speaking* only in this book, rather than writing or reading, we will not focus too much on this. Just note the concept of *elision*, dropping a vowel when two vowels appear together. It is something you will have to learn as you continue your French education!

Cultural note: France is a large country with many different regions. The food of France changes depending on where you are. If you visit Lorraine, you might try their famous *quiche*. Aquitaine is well known for its *foie gras*, fattened duck or goose liver. No matter where you travel in France, you will be sure to find delicious food!

Idea! Let your kids brag! Encourage them to tell Grandma, or their teacher, or friend that they know the days of the week and the months of the year. Every time they use their French to communicate (even to brag a little) they are learning more of the language!

Week 31: When Is Your Birthday?

Review: Week 29: Months of the Year

Vocabulary:

Quand est ton anniversaire?　　(When is your birthday?)
kahn-ay-ton-an-nee-vehr-sayr

Mon anniversaire est en ......　　(My birthday is in.....)
mon an-nee-vehr-sayr-ee-than

Grammar note: Here we are using the familiar form of your, *ton*. You would probably know someone fairly well if you were asking them their birthday! If you were asking a teacher, for example, you would use the formal your, *votre*.

Cultural note: The French have created some delicious desserts as well as healthy meals! Some French desserts are *tarte tatin*, an upside down tart, *crème brulée*, a custard, and *profiteroles*, a cream puff. A sweet treat French children might enjoy at a birthday party is the same one children love all over the world...Gummy Bears!

Idea! If your child's birthday is between 1-10 let them try to figure out how they would say the date of their birth: *"Mon anniversaire est le 4 juillet"*. If their birthday is a bigger number, help them look up the number and figure it out!

Week 32: Review

- Learning all this useful information requires a lot of memorization.

  o Use playing cards or preschool counting flashcards to review numbers.
  o Count cars on the road. How many...trucks, red cars, motorcycles, etc.
  o Practice your days of the week song or create your own.
  o Try some fun games and videos available online. I like the games on digitaldialects.com/french and bbc.co.uk/schools/primarylanguages/french
  o Have a group birthday party. Bake profiteroles or another tasty French treat. Everyone has to state their birthday in order to get a taste.

- Learn more about the food of France

  o Try feeding your children an afternoon goûter.
  o Visit a French bakery.
  o Structure a dinner the French way, course by course.
  o Enjoy a croissant for breakfast.
  o Introduce your child to some vegetables that are seldom used in North America, like endive, fennel or celery root.

Unit 5: Mealtimes

Week 33: I'm Hungry

Review: Concepts from Weeks 25-32

Vocabulary:

> Tu as faim? (Are you hungry?)
> *too-ah-fahn*

> J'ai faim.   (I'm hungry.)
> *jhee-fahn*

Grammar note: In French, when we answer a question in the negative, the word no is expressed as *ne pas.*

Example: *Tu as faim?   Non. Je n'ai pas faim.*

A contraction is used to express the word *ne*. If this is too confusing, you can stick with a simple, *Non.*

Cultural note: Gustave Eiffel was the designer of the famous Eiffel Tower. In 1889, when it was built, it was the tallest structure in the world!

Idea! This is one of the easiest conversations to practice because we all have meals every day! Incorporate this simple question into your regular mealtimes.

Week 34: Favorite Foods

Review: Week 33: I'm Hungry

Vocabulary:

le pain   (bread)
luh pehn

la pomme   (apple)
lah pohm

la confiture   (jam)
lah kohn-fee-choor

le fromage   (cheese)
luh froh-mahj

les biscuits   (cookies)
lay bee-swee

les carottes   (carrots)
lay-cahr-eht

Pronunciation note: Remember, in French the consonants at the end of the word are often not pronounced.

Cultural note: Have you ever watched the movie *The Hunchback of Notre Dame*? It is based on a very famous book of the same name written by Victor Hugo. In France they call the book, *Notre Dame de Paris*

Idea! Brainstorm your own list of favorite foods. Your kids will learn their own favorites quicker if they have to ask for them in French in order to receive them!

Week 35: I Like......

Review: Week 34: Favorite Foods
Vocabulary:

> Est-ce que tu aimes.. (Do you like...?)
> *Ehs-kuh-too-ehm...*
>
> J'aime   (I like....)
> *jhehm*

Grammar note: *Aimes* and *aime* are two forms of the verb aimer, which means, to like. In French, the verb changes depending on who or what it is referring to.

Cultural note: Louis Braille invented the series of raised dots that enable visually impaired people from all over the world to read. His system is used in almost every country in the world.

Idea! You can have a lot of fun practicing this concept. Tell the children they are having horrible things for breakfast, lunch, or dinner and innocently ask them, *"Est-ce que tu aimes?"* They can respond with an emphatic, *"Non!"*

Week 36: I'm Thirsty!

Review: Week 33: I'm Hungry!

Vocabulary:

> Tu as soif ?   (Are you thirsty?)
> *oo-ah-swahf*

> J'ai soif.   (I'm thirsty.)
> *jhee-swahf*

Grammar note: The phrase, *"Tu as soif?"* literally means *"Do you have thirst?"*. Similarly, *"J'ai soif."* means, *"I have thirst."* This is yet another example of why we translate for meaning, not word for word.

Cultural note: Coco Chanel was born very poor in 1883, grew up in an orphanage and was taught to sew. She took those skills and became the most influential fashion designer of the twentieth century. Her business empire lasts to this day, still including her signature perfume, suits and little black dress.

Idea! A hot summer's day is a great time to make a pitcher of lemonade and see who is thirsty. Weather not warm? Try and make some hot cocoa instead!

Week 37: Can I Have......?

Review: Week 34: Favorite Foods

Vocabulary:

Je voudrais____, s'il vous plaît.   (I would like_____please?)
jhay-voo-drah-oon-beeskweet-see-voo-play

Grammar note: As in English, there are more than one ways to request things in French. Just like in English, it is important to ask politely, adding *s'il vous plaît*.

Cultural note: Jacques Cousteau was a French inventor, photographer and scientist. He became famous all over the world for his work exploring and documenting ocean life. He produced television shows that exposed people to the mysteries of the deep ocean.

Idea! Make snack time practice time! Let your children pick their own afternoon *goûter* and then ask for it – *en français*-of course!

Week 38: Sit at the Table

Review: Week 37: Can I Have…?

Vocabulary:

> À table!   (Sit at the table.)
> *ah-tahbl*

Pronunciation note: The *l* sound in *table* is very subtle, not like the strong "l" sound we produce when we say "table".

Cultural note: France has produced so many influential artists, but one of the most famous is Pierre-Auguste Renoir. Renoir's painting are characterized by vibrant, colorful and realistic images

Idea! Assign a "dinner helper" who gets the rest of the family to the table each night. Pick a different dinner helper every night so each child gets a chance to practice using and listening to this command.

Week 39: Where Is My.....?

Review: Week 38: Sit Down at the Table.

Vocabulary:

> la tasse   (cup)
> *lah-tahs*
>
> la fourchette (fork)
> *lah-foorjh*
>
> le couteau   (knife)
> *luh-kwuh-too*
>
> la cuillère   (spoon)
> *lah-kyee-yair*
>
> et   (and)
> *ay*

Pronunciation note: Remember the word *et* is pronounced like the English sound, ay.

Cultural note: No one like getting a shot at the doctor! However, thanks to the scientific work developed by French scientist Louis Pasteur, people all over the world have become safe from diseases such as anthrax, cholera and smallpox.

Idea! Pair up different items you have previously learned using your new word *et*. Play *Maman dit* with two items instead of one.

Example: *Maman dit, "Touche ton nez et ta bouche"*.

Week 40: Review

- Mealtime vocabulary is some of the easiest vocabulary to learn. Practice times occur every day so it feels easy and natural to incorporate these words. In addition, children enjoy learning and using the names of their favorite foods.

  - At a restaurant, see if you can translate any items on the menu.
  - Mix your old vocabulary with new. When asked, "Comment ça va?" you can respond, "J'ai faim". You can use the phrase, "Où est ...?" to locate food items on the table.

- Learn more about some famous French people!

  - Visit your local library and take out biographies on famous French citizens. There are too many to name!
  - Go to biography.com to find a wide selection of stories about men, women and children from France.

- Although the contributions the French have made in science, literature, world affairs and music is considerable, their impact on the art world is indescribable. Consider visiting your local museum to locate works by French artists.

Unit 6: Getting Ready

Week 41: Wake Up!

Review: Vocabulary and concepts from weeks 32-39.

Vocabulary:

> Réveille-toi!   (Wake up!)
> *rehv-ay-toh-ah*

> Bonjour, mon enfant! (Good morning ,my child!)
> *bohn-jhoor-mohn-ahn-fahn*

Grammar note: Sometimes in French, we add the pronoun directly to the verb. Here we are literally saying, "Wake yourself!"

Cultural note: French is not only spoken in France! French is the official language in 29 different countries around the world. Most of these countries speak languages other than French as well, but the influence of France has influenced their language and society.

Idea! Start your day in French! Wake your children every day with a cheery, *"Réveille-toi! Bonjour, mon enfant!"*.

Week 42: Getting Ready

Review: Week 41: Wake Up!

Vocabulary:

> Je me lave le visage.   (I wash my face.)
> *jhay-may-lahv-lay-veesahj*

> Je me brosse les dents.   (I brush my teeth.)
> *jhay-may-bruhs-lay-dahn*

> Je m'habille.   (I get dressed.)
> *jhay-may-beel*

Grammar: When we are writing or speaking about parts of the body we use the articles *le* or *la* instead of the pronoun *mon or ma.*

Cultural note: France once had colonies in Africa. These former colonies are now independent countries, but they still have many French aspects, including speaking French. Some of these countries are: Algeria, Senegal and Morocco.

Idea! Have your child tell you what he has to do in the morning before he leaves for school or otherwise starts his day.

Week 43: I Want To Wear.....(A)

Review: Week 42: Getting Ready

Vocabulary:

Je veux porter...... *jhay-voo-pohr-tayr*	(I want to wear....)
un tee-shirt *ahn-tee-shirt*	(tee shirt)
un pantalon *ahn-pahn-tah-lohn*	(pants)
une robe *uhn rohb*	(dress)
une jupe *uhn jhewp*	(skirt)
un short *ahn-short*	(shorts)

Grammar note: Remember number agreement. You must match your pronoun or article to your noun.

Cultural note: Morocco is an African country located on the coast of the Mediterranean Sea. The people of Morocco speak Arabic, but French remains the language of business.

Idea! Before you put your kids to bed, help them pick out their outfits using their French vocabulary.

Week 44: I Want To Wear ...(B)

Review: Week 43: I Want To Wear....(A)

Vocabulary:

du rose *rohz*	(pink)
du rouge *roojh*	(red)
du bleu(e) *bluh*	(blue)
du vert(e) *vair(vairt)*	(green)
du blanc(he) *blahn (blahnsh)*	(white)
du noir(e) *nwahr*	(black)
de l'orange *oh-rahnjh*	(orange)
du jaune *jhohn*	(yellow)
du violet(te) *vee-oh-lay (vee-oh-leht)*	(purple)

Grammar note: The words for some colors in French have different endings when they are used with a masculine or a feminine noun. The changes have been noted above.

Cultural note: Belgium is a small country that shares a border with France. French is one of their three official languages, along with Dutch and German. Belgium is a kingdom..with a real king and royal family!

Idea! Play *I Spy* using your new color words. Of course, when we are studying French we don't play *I Spy* we play *Je vois quelque chose*.... (I see something...).

Week 45: Where Are Your Shoes?

Review: Week 44: I Want To Wear…(B).

Vocabulary:

> Où sont tes chaussures?   (Where are your shoes?)
> *whee-sohn-tay-shahtoor*

> Les voici!   (Here they are!)
> *lay-vah-see*

Pronunciation note: The French *ch* is pronounced like the English *sh*.

Cultural note: Switzerland is another small European country that uses French as one of its four official languages. Switzerland is a neutral country, which means it never takes sides in any war, and remains peaceful.

Idea! Hide some everyday items and make the phrase, *Où sont..?* the start of a treasure hunt!

Week 46: Let's Hurry Up!

Review: Weeks 2 and 6: Greetings

Vocabulary:

> Dépêche-toi!   (Let's hurry up!)
> *Day-pehsh-twah*

Grammar note: Dépêche-toi is used when you are talking to one person. If you need to hustle your whole family out the door, say, *Dépêchez-vous (day-pehsh-voo)*!

Cultural note: Québec (pronounced *kay bek*) is the largest province in Canada and almost all people there speak French. The province is larger than Alaska and contains Canada's second biggest city, Montreal.

Idea! Give each child a turn to sound the morning alarm. Let them announce, *Dépêchez-vous!* Maybe it will help get you out of the house on time!

Week 47: Have a Good Day!

Review: Week 46: It's Time to Go!

Vocabulary:

> Bonne journée!   (Have a nice day!)
> *buhn jhoor-nay*

Pronunciaton note: *Bonne* (*buhn*) is pronounced differently than *Bon (bahn)*.

Cultural note: New Orleans is a city in Louisiana that retains much of its French culture. Some residents speak *Cajun French* or *Creole French*, different types of North American French.

Idea! Find a French restaurant and get lunch. Make sure to wish the waiter, " *Bonne journée!* ".

Week 48: Review

- Review all the vocabulary and concepts from the past weeks.

  - Incorporate your new vocabulary when getting
  - dressed every day.
  - Pretend! Play puppets, paper dolls or Barbies with your kids and use your French vocabulary to get them dressed.
  - Label clothing you see in stores when you are out
  - shopping.

- Learn more about French culture around the world!

  - Make a book out of the flags of French influenced countries
  - Listen to some French-African music. There are many varieties!
  - "Pin" a map! Get a world map, and help your child put a pushpin into all the countries where French is spoken around the world.
  - Watch a Mardi Gras Parade on Youtube.com
  - Google images of the majestic Alps, the mountain range that separates France from some if its French speaking neighbors.

Unit 7: A Few Odds and Ends

Week 49: Things Around the House

Review: Vocabulary from Weeks 41-47

Vocabulary:

> le lit   (bed)
> *luh-lee*
>
> le canapé   (sofa)
> *luh-kah-nah-pay*
>
> la lampe   (lamp)
> *lah lahmp*
>
> le téléphone   (telephone)
> *luh-tay-lay-fohn*
>
> l'ordinateur   (computer)
> *lohr-deen-ah-tewr*

Pronunciation note: When you see the letter *eur* together, you pronounce the sound like *yoor*.

Cultural note: Do you like fairy tales? Many well known stories have come from French author Charles Perrault. He wrote *Cinderella, Sleeping Beauty* and *Puss in Boots*.

Idea! Play *¿Chaud ou Froid?* (Hot or Cold?). Play the same way you would play Hot or Cold? But instead of hiding an item, you simply think of one in the room and direct your children toward it by saying *chaud* or *froid*. When they find it they have to tell you what it is in French. Then they get a turn!

Week 50: Things in Our World.

Review: Week 21: Who Is This?

Vocabulary:

Qu'est-ce que c'est? (What is this?)
Keh-skeh-uh-say

le bus   (bus)
luh-boos

la voiture   (car)
lah-vwah-tewr

le ciel   (sky)
luh-see-yehl

la rue   (street)
lah-rew

les gens   (people)
lay-jhuh

le train   (train)
luh-trahn

la rivière   (river)
lah-ree-vee-ayr

la fleur   (flower)
luh-flewr

l'arbre   (tree)
luh-ahrb

Grammar note: If you want to say *the*, you use *le* or *la*.

If you want to say *a*, you use *un* or *une*.

Example: C'est une fleur. = It is a flower.

C'est la fleur. = It is the flower.

Cultural note: France is sometimes referred to as L'Hexagone because is shaped like a hexagon!

Idea! Use the question, *Qu'est-ce que c'est?* to practice mixing up you articles and pronouns. Try different ways of answering the same question:

It is my car/ It is the car. *C'est ma voiture./ C'est la voiture.*

It is a train/It is the train. *C'est un train./C'est le train.*

Week 51: Places We Go

Review: Week 50: Things in Our World

Vocabulary:

Allons (à)....... (Let's go to.....)
ahl-lohn-uh

l'école   (school)
lay-kohl

le restaurant   (restaurant)
luh-rehs-tuh-rahn

la boutique   (store)
lah-boo-teek

la plage   (beach)
lah-plahjh

le parc   (park)
luh-park

les films   (movies)
lay-feelm

la banque   (bank)
lah-bahnk

Grammar note: *Boutique* is one of the many French words that has been adopted into our English vocabulary. Conversely, *les films* is an English word that has been adopted by the French!

Cultural note: France is the only country in Europe that has a Disneyland.

Idea! Make running errands a learning experience. Narrate where you are headed as you run around town and let your kids translate before you get there!

Week 52: Review

- Review your vocabulary from weeks 49-51.
- Have a fête! You did it! A year of studying a foreign language is no small feat. Plan a party for you and your children. Incorporate some of the foods and customs you have learned about over the past year. Don't be afraid to mix and match!
- Keep practicing your French vocabulary. The more you speak, the more you will retain.
- Keep learning! Read French language storybooks. Listen to French songs and music. Hopefully you have embarked on a love affair with this new language. Keep your curiosity piqued and bring your children along for the ride!

Where Do I Go From Here?

Here you are, a year or so later with a good deal of spoken vocabulary in your pocket. What's next? That question can only be answered by you. The key to mastering any language is to continue speaking it. No amount of studying can make you fluent if you don't reach out to others and try to communicate. Continue to make learning French a family affair. You will always have study buddies and you will be giving your children a priceless gift. Utilize the internet to find others who are interested in practicing their French. Join social groups and take daily opportunities to use the French you have already obtained.

For more formal instruction, you can register for inexpensive courses online through any number of companies. There are many companies operating out of French speaking countries that offer lessons through Skype for just a few dollars a lesson. Also available online are courses through the Alliance Française, a nonprofit organization whose goal is to promote French language and culture internationally. The contact information is noted in the following section.

Many libraries have audio and computer courses available to lend. Some libraries even offer French/English tutoring classes. This is a great way to meet native French speakers, improve your spoken French, and help someone at the same time.

Another affordable option is to attend local community French courses for adult learners. Most communities offer seasonal enrichment courses, and Beginner's French is very often one of the choices. You may meet other people interested in learning French with whom you can practice.

If you are very goal oriented, or want to receive certification of some sort, you can attend classes at a community college where you live. This will certainly increase your knowledge of written French. Course offerings vary and usually don't extend beyond beginner-intermediate levels. If you want to delve deeper into the language, you can set the long term goal of receiving your DELF/DALF diplomas. These are internationally recognized diplomas granted by the French Ministry of Education. You can list the degree on your resume if you are learning French for professional reasons. It is also quite a personal accomplishment!

There are so many free resources available nowadays online that you can easily continue your French language learning on your own time . The next section outlines many free resources you can use to increase your French skills.

Learning Resources

All websites, smart phone applications and podcasts listed below are available for free. Books and music should be available at most local libraries.

Internet Sites

familylanguageresources.com: A collection of links to free learning websites, free lesson plans, free worksheets and curriculum to pace your instruction. The site also has a section of reviewed learning materials; books, cds and curriculum packages

YouTube.com: We all love youtube.com for funny emails but it really is an invaluable teaching resource when you want to learn about or expose your children to different cultures.

googletranslate.com: Hit this site for quick general translations.

livemocha.com: Do you like Facebook? This site is designed to promote communication with language learners all over the world. You can email or chat with members in English or French. Complimentary lessons are available. You can also earn "money" towards fee based lessons by correcting the lessons of English language learners. In addition, great pictures taken by locals of foreign countries all over the world are available for viewing in the "Explore Culture" section.

bbc.co.uk/schools/primarylanguages/French: This is a terrific site for children. French vocabulary is divided up into topics.

Explanations are provided for each topic, and corresponding games are available to reinforce learning.

digitaldialects.com: This site presents a selection of fun, engaging French vocabulary building games.

earlystart.co.uk: This is a great site for finding supplementary information while your children learn about France and the French language. The information is broken down into topics like "Greetings" and "Pets" so it is easy to look for information you need.

ToLearnFrench.com: This is a comprehensive website compiled by a French teacher in France. Here you may find lesson plans, tests, and dialogues. You can also join the site and get a French penpal.

Apps

MindSnacks Learn French has some really fun games if you want to develop your visual knowledge of the French language. Oral presentation of words is also included with a native accent.

iTranslate is a great feature to keep on your phone. If you want to add to your personal repertoire, or are trying to have small conversations with native speakers, you just type in the word you want to say and it gives you a translation. You can also hit an icon next to the phrase to hear it spoken with proper pronunciation.

Duolingo is an app containing great vocabulary and grammar building games. You can slow down the speed to make the words easier to understand.

Podcasts

Listening to podcasts in French is a great way to improve your understanding of spoken language.

Of interest to adults:

Coffee break French is another terrific resource for boosting your listening comprehension, and achieving verbal skills. This is a course consisting of eighty short lessons that are aimed at beginners. You can access this free course through iTunes or go to their website at radiolingua.com/shows/coffee-break-french.

Newsinslowfrench.com: This site's title sums it up. Current news is provided in French at a slower speed. Free vocabulary flashcards accompany each weeks report, There are a number of free demo lessons available, and a student subscription is inexpensive.

For children:

Podbean.com: This site provides stories in French for children, spoken by children. There are a great variety of podcasts to choose from.

Thefrenchexperiment.com: This site has translated familiar stories that are read aloud by a native French speaker. Translations are provided. This is a great opportunity for your child to hear a proper accent model.

Books

Usborne Books is a publishing company that has created many bright, colorful and interactive French language books for children. Some of their titles are aimed at the youngest children, and contain interactive features like lift-a-flap. Other books are designed to engage older children. Check out their complete selection of titles at myubam.com. Many local libraries carry their books.

Play and Learn French (McGraw-Hill, 2005) by Ana Lomba and Marcela Summerville contains some fun rhymes and short stories you can read aloud to your children and decipher meaning together. Translations are provided and the illustrations are vibrant and engaging.

Merriam- Webster's classic *French-English, English-French Dictionary* is a handy resource to have around the house. Should your conversations with your children lead you to a place that is not covered in this book, you will be able to find most of the language you need in this comprehensive guide.

Music

Using CD's in the car is great for listening comprehension.

Let's Sing and Dance in French by French Songs for Kids is a fun selection of French music suitable for preschool and elementary school age kids.

Fun French for Kids by Beth Manners contains songs and stories easy enough for your youngest children to follow along.

Did you enjoy *52 Weeks of Family French*? Please share the fun!

Go to the Facebook page,
www.facebook.com/52weeksoffamilyspanish
Give the book a "like" to spread the word! You will also find links to other great Spanish learning activities. I am always on the prowl for fun, easy and effective French activities so the page is updated frequently. Keep checking in!

"Pin" the book on www.pinterest.com and all your followers will get a chance to see the book.

Have a free moment? I am always grateful for reviews on www.amazon.com.

Thanks for reading and keep your eyes open for *Color Me French!*, due out November 2012.

ABOUT THE AUTHOR

Eileen Mc Aree is a teacher, writer and mother. She lives in New York with her husband, four kids and their dog, Biscuit.